Divine Comedy of Neophyte Corax and Goddess Morrigan.
A dialectic play.

Payam Nabarz

'Web of Wyrd Press'
An Imprint of BECS Ltd.

1

Divine Comedy of Neophyte Corax and Goddess Morrigan.
A dialectic play

By Payam Nabarz

Published in 2008 by 'Web of Wyrd Press'
An imprint of BECS Ltd.
http://www.myspace.com/webofwyrdpress

Some of the acts in this play were first published in 2003 in Touchstone magazine and online.

ISBN-13: 978-0-9556858-0-4

Disclaimer: All places, events and all characters in this play are fictitious and any resemblance to any one alive or dead is purely accidental.

Author Biography:

Payam Nabarz is author of *'The Mysteries of Mithras: The Pagan Belief That Shaped the Christian World'* (Inner Traditions, 2005), and *'The Persian Mar Nameh: The Zoroastrian Book of the Snake Omens & Calendar'* (Twin Serpents, 2006). He is the editor of the *'Mithras Readers: an*

academic and religious journal of Greek, Roman and Persian Studies' (Twin Serpents, 2006).

He is the founder of *Spirit of Peace*, a charitable organisation dedicated to personal inner peace and world peace via interfaith dialogue between different spiritual paths.

Nabarz's writings have appeared in numerous esoteric magazines including Touchstone (the Journal of Order of Bards, Ovates, Druids), Pagan Dawn (the Journal of the Pagan Federation), Stone Circle, The Little Red Book, Pentacle, White Dragon, Silver Star, Cauldron, and the Sufi.

For further information: http://www.myspace.com/nabarz

Table of content
Acts I-XIV.

Acknowledgements: 6

Preface   7

Act I Lammas.   9

Act II: The Autumnal Equinox   16

Act III: Samhain.   21

Act IV: The Winter Solstice- Alban Arthan: the birth of the sun.   26

Act V: A Kali Puja: a magickal workshop.   31

Act VI: Imbolc   37

Act VII: The Dance of Death   39

Act VIII Beltane 4play   42

Act IX: An eclectic pagan's near-death experience   44

Act X: Beltane   48

Act XI: Justice for the RollRight Stone Circle   49

Act XII: Living like the pagan ancestors   50

Act XIII: The Towers of Silence   52

Act XIV: The Magi's gifts   56

Q: 'Are you here of your own free will or by compulsion?'- Baba Yaga
A: 'Largely of my own free will, and twice as much by compulsion!'- Ivan

Acknowledgements:

Parts of some Wiccan, Thelemic, and Druid ritual materials have been included here.

The 'Hail unto thee, who art Tum in Thy setting ...' is from *Liber Resh vel Helios sub figura CC* by Aleister Crowley for details *see Magick in Theory and Practice* (Red Wheel/Weiser, 1994) p645.

'We die from a mineral state and reach a plant state' is a Rumi Sufi poem, see *The last barrier a Sufi journey* by Reshad Feild (Elements Books 1990), p39.

The 'Farewell O Sun, ever returning Light...' and 'Dread lord of shadows, god of life, giver of life...' and 'Queen of the moon, Queen of the Sun...' are from the *Wiccan Book of Shadows*.

The hymn 'I see my line of ancestors' is based on a last rite hymn in the film the *13th Warrior*. For a more exact translation of the hymn see *Ibn Fadlans' journey to Russia: a tenth-century traveller from Baghdad to the Volga River* by Prof Richard Frye (Markus Wiener, 2006) p69.

To Alison Jones for reading this manuscript and her numerous helpful comments.

All the photographs inside the book were taken by Payam Nabarz.

The Raven painting on first page is by an unknown artist.

Cover skull artwork by Lulu.com

Every effort has been made to trace holders of copyrights. Any inadvertent omissions of acknowledgement or permission can be rectified in future editions.

For further information: http://www.myspace.com/nabarz

Preface

A pagan religion of the Romans, Mithraism, much favoured among soldiers, involved initiates wearing a raven head-mask and wings. Such a cult-follower was called *Corax*, which is now the zoological name for the raven — *Corvus corax*.

Ravens are reminders of death. Birds of ill-omen, they feed off the dead, human or animal. No doubt the hacked flesh of battlefields ensured the presence of ravens, which became associated with disaster in the same way as vultures are in other parts of the world. Indeed, like vultures, they may hasten death by taking out the eyes and tongue and then proceed to tear open the abdomen, operations for which their sharp and powerful beaks are well suited.

In medieval times, the bodies or bits of bodies of executed prisoners were displayed in public on spikes or in iron cages on the turrets and battlements of the Tower as a warning to all. Ravens would take their gory pickings.

A chronicler of the time recorded the execution of a traitor in 1283: after being hanged, drawn and quartered, "the villain's head was bound with iron, lest it should fall to pieces from putrefaction, and set conspicuously upon a long spear-shaft for the mockery of London." Twenty years later, his head, with that of his brother alongside, could be seen, picked clean.

Today, the ravens are fed and cared for by the Yeoman Ravenmaster. He is regarded by them as a raven himself in a very real way, for he has reared them. Only he can approach the ravens closely or handle them. The ravens are guarding their territory and they will attack you should you come within reach, so be warned:

RAVENS ARE DANGEROUS!

Plaque at Tower of London shows and desribes a Corax grade initiate in Roman Cult of Mithras. A Raven in Tower of London, according to legends if these protector Ravens leave the Tower of London the kingdom will fall.

7

One who is Three

Morrigan
Goddess of War,
bestower and reaper of life
Phantom Queen.

Black-feathered, spear in hand
naked breasts heavy with blood and milk,
standing across the river of life.

Your beloved die in your arms,
your foes die at your feet.
Dark mother, luscious Crone, Goddess of death

as a battle rages,
your are there, graceful Raven
tearing flesh from bone.

As the moon wanes
we become closer, and closer
at the dark moon;
we dance in your cave.
Great Queen, Morrigan.

Nabarz - April 1997.

Act I Lammas.

Scene I

Somewhere inside a great nest, on top of a very tall tree, in the centre of a magical landscape.

Corax: Great Raven Goddess, what mystery lies at the heart of Lammas?

Morrigan: Go away, can't you see I am eating?

Corax: Yes, it's the offering I have brought you.

Morrigan: Ok, just go away, come back when I have finished.

Corax: I can't really walk away, the offering was my leg, which you are eating.

Morrigan: Ok just shut up and wait here until I finish eating your offering and then I will answer your question.

Corax: Well, I can't wait until you finish eating to get the answer to my question.

Morrigan: Why not?

Corax: Well my leg is still attached to me.

Morrigan: So?

Corax: Well by the time you finish eating, there will be nothing of me left to hear your answer.

Morrigan: Bloody impatient humans, it's all now, now and now. I can't even finish my lunch without complaints, if you wanted answers you should have gone to Buddha, he is in the big house on the hill; but no, you climbed the tree into MY nest.

Corax: OK I'll just keep quiet till you finish.

Crunch, crunch, crunch; slowly Corax finds himself in the belly of the Raven Goddess. After the bones are pecked clean, some strange feeling engulfs him, while floating above his own skeleton. The Raven Goddess looks directly at him and says: "Thanks for the lunch, well I am going for a nap."

If Corax had a body he might have been bothered by this or stamped his foot, but in his current ethereal state, there was not much that could be done.

Many sunsets later, the Raven Goddess wakes up, and begins to stretch her wings across the sky blocking the sun briefly. Faced with a pile of human and animal skeletons in her nest, she does bit of spring cleaning; she picks the remains off, carries them to a field, and buries them. If Corax still had a consciousness, he might have noticed four strange creatures that were based in each corner of the field.

Scene II.

A Great Bear stands at the North, whose head is among the stars and feet deep in caves of the earth. In the East flies a Hawk with the colours of dawn behind it. In the South running across the edge of the field is a Stag with fiery red eyes. In the West in a never ending pool swims a Salmon. Once the Raven Goddess flies off leaving the skeletons behind, the four continue their conservation.

North: The Raven has placed more bones in my caves.

East: I know it is time to begin again.

West: We must not be distracted from our task, Lugh is almost complete.

South: Yes, let's focus on that task; these new bones will grow alongside Lugh.

North: In the night of the year, the Land lay bare.

East: In the dawn of the year, buds burst, shoots sprouted.

South: In the noon of the year, flowers bloomed, petals blossomed.

West: Now is the day of harvest. Ripe fruit falls; the golden corn is cut in the ear.

East: Remember as we harvest, that we shall be the harvest in the field of stars.

South: At midday the golden lord is sacrificed in his strength. His glory is the fire. This is Light.

West: In the evening His body is washed for its wounds by she who loved him. His healing is in the Waters. This is Love.

North: At night his form is laid deep in the lap of the Land. His transformation is in the Earth. This is Liberty.

East: In the morning the Child of Light is born from his mother. His renewal is in the air. This is Life.

All: The union of the four directions is: Light, Life, Love, Liberty.

West: Death and glory, healing, transformation and renewal; this is the journey of the seed; and the seed is Spirit.

From seed to ripe to corn, to flour and water to bread. We also transform and change like grapes to wine in the vat.

We die from a mineral state and reach a plant state;
And from plants we die and became animals.

We die from our animal state and became humans.
Then why fear disappearance through death?
Next time we shall die
We will bring forth wings and feathers like angels;
Next, soaring higher than angels
What you can not imagine,
We shall be that.

As Lugh is raised, so are all the bones that were laid in the
field, all the seeds came up, including the bones of the curious
Corax, who now almost understood the mystery of Lammas.

Scene III.

Time passes and Corax is sitting in front of the Great Raven Goddess once more, fully intact but this time he also has a new pair of black wings.

Morrigan: You again? What now?

Corax: Well, I was wondering about the mysteries of the Autumnal Equinox

Morrigan: *grins* Ok if you insist, have you tried swimming in the Western seas before?

Corax: No, as I don't how to swim.

Morrigan: *bigger grin* Well the answer lies at bottom of the ocean.

Corax: But I don't swim! (*The sea approaches very quickly*) *Ahhhhhhgh ... SPLASH.*

Morrigan: You don't need to swim, just sink into the bottom.

Corax: Blob, blob....

Act II: The Autumnal Equinox

Scene I.

Corax *begins his descent into the Western ocean, slowly sinking into the bottom, as his eyes get used to the dark, he notices lots of other creatures also descending.*

Corax: Hello there!

Silence

Corax: Anyone living here?

A voice replies: In Silence is the seed of wisdom gained.

Suddenly the water around him becomes alive with electricity, and the same **voice says:** You who still are alive, why are you approaching the land of the eternal youth?

Corax: My name is Corax and great Raven Goddess has dropped me in it again! All I asked was that I wanted to know more about the Autumnal Equinox. Who are you?

Voice: My name is Modron , so my sister has brought here to see the Light of Water; the Alban Elued?

Corax: Yes, strangely as I began my fall from the sky, I noticed the sun was setting in the west and into the sea. But it's all dark here!

Modron: My sun is within me, and now my realm approaches the land of the living.

Corax: Is your realm all the waters of the world?

Modron: Yes and my sun returns to me every year. All of your kind knew this once, the Egyptians called me Isis and sometimes at sunset, facing west, they would say: goddess Auramoth, Hail unto thee, who art Tum in Thy setting, even unto Thee who art Tum in Thy joy, who travellest over the Heavens in Thy bark at the Down-going of the Sun. Tahuti standeth in his splendour at the prow, and Ra-Hoor abideth at the helm. Hail unto to Thee from the Abodes of Day!. While for the Persians Autumn Equinox saw the beginning of their month of Mehr (Mithra), and start of the festival of Mehragan. As well as remembering my son and lover Mithra they remembered me too and the month of the sun god Mithra was followed by my month; month of the Sea Goddess Anahita (Aban). The month of the sun leads into the month of the sea, which is like its Druid equivalent (Alban Elued) the sun beings setting into the ocean. The sunset over the ocean is one of the most beautiful sights there is, as the sun unites with the ocean, the light is reflected upon the water. That is Mehr coming together with Aban, giving rise to a third Persian word: 'Mehraban', which translates as kindness/one who is kind. The child of light, is the Mabon who comes out of the union between Sun and Sea and is 'Kindness'.

Corax: But I thought the Mabon is known as the Great Prisoner, the Great Son who was taken away from his mother Modron three nights after his birth, and has been the goal of many spiritual quests. Why are you keeping the Mabon prisoner? The child of eternal light needs to come out after being hidden in the sea? Why is he your son?

Modron: *laughter* He is not a prisoner! I give birth to ALL, males and females, my daughter is my daughter and son is my son. The Mabon is the Inner Light within all of my children and all life. While the child is born at the Winter Solstice, the time of Autumn Equinox belongs to him, and people say farewell to him. As he goes through the gates of death and harvest, he is within the seed of plants and the seed of light in all. The Mabon is fire and water, Sun and Sea in Union, creating what you seek: the most important spiritual quality, that of 'kindness'.

Corax: Blob, blob...

Modron: Oh dear, you seemed a bit shocked by what I have told as you seem to have gone a bit blue and your eyes are a bit red.

Corax: No I am not shocked, it's just that I don't have any gills.

Modron: Foolish bird, you are drowning, you shouldn't be swimming; you are meant to fly! Right, let's take you to a place where the water is thinner and you can breathe.

Scene II.

The water becomes less fluid and feels more like mist than water, Corax looks around, above his head there is still water, so they are still deep within the ocean, but it is not dark, and the golden colours of the sun are shimmering all around.

Modron: This is isle of Avalon, hidden deep within my womb. Stay here until you regain your colour and breath, then fly out fast, it's not your time to stay here.

Corax flies towards the nearest tree, which is an apple tree, and begins to dry his feathers and breathes deeply. Under the tree he sees four familiar creatures. A Great Bear stands at the North, whose head is among the stars and feet deep in caves of the earth. In the East flies a Hawk with the colours of dawn behind it. In the South running across the edge of the field is a Stag with fiery red eyes. In the west in a never ending pool swims a Salmon. The four animals are speaking to each other.

West: Farewell O Sun, ever returning Light,

North: The hidden god who ever yet remains, who now departs to the land of Youth, through the Gates of Death, to dwell enthroned; the judge of gods and men.

East: The Horned leader of the hosts of the Air, even as he stands unseen about the Circle.

South: So dwelt He, within the secret Seed, the seed of the newly reaped grain, the seed of flesh, hidden in earth, the marvellous seed of the Stars.

West: In him is Life and Light is the life of Man, that which was never born and never dies, therefore the wise ones weep not, but rejoice.

As Corax finally flies out of the sea, he is wondering to himself about the stag, the bear, the salmon and the hawk. What do they do for fun? They all seem to be so serious every time he meets them.

Morrigan: So you're looking for fun?

Corax: No, I was just wondering!

Morrigan: Well, it means you're beginning to take yourself too seriously. Lets see, I think I need to turn you to into a Korrigan for a while and have fun.....

So with that, a transformation occurs from Corax to a Korrigan; a Celtic fairy son.

20

Act III: Samhain.

Scene I.
A smoke and incense filled room, candles are burning, a group of people are drinking and smoking, music is playing in the background.

Corax has his wings folded, and is sitting next to a Fox on a couch. A blackbird with shiny wings is rolling a joint. A red Dragon is cutting few lines of coke on glass table. A hawk is arranging a pile of stones in shape of a circle, rain is falling in through the window and sound of a storm can be heard outside. Rowan, Ash, and Oak trees seem to be growing in the room and holly and ivy are climbing the walls. The walls themselves are transparent, the southern wall leads to an Egyptian temple, the eastern wall leads to a Hindu temple, the

Western wall leads to a Druid Grove , and the Northern wall leads to a Viking hall. Looking at the walls one sees into each of the temples, filled with busy worshippers in a different time and place. With another puff on the spliff, Corax feels even more light headed, he lies on his back looking at the ceiling, which is also transparent and the star filled night sky and moon are visible.

Giant black wings block out the moon and the stars and a **voice says:** Corax, are you feeling ok?

Corax: Yes fine, though not sure where my body is. Is that you Great Queen Raven?

Morrigan: No it's a earth worm! Of course it's me, who else has giant black wings, the sun as one eye and the moon as the other eye, duh! What have you been doing? Has being a Korrighan suited you?

Corax:
From the Coven to the Zodiac, the flash of disco lights,
the constant beat of goth and trance sets my mind alight.
I became a dancing Korrigan,
a child of childless Morrigan.

Music sets your body on fire,
the dance floor an Agoris bonefire.
I became a freakish Korrigan,
A furious hound of Morrigan.

Don't be such a f**king prude,
When you need to be rather crude.
I became a love-mad Korrigan,
Not Cuchulainn sparing thy Morrigan.

In leather, lace or Sari, reach for state of Zar,
Shiva, Isis or Pan, thy goal is not far.
I became a nocturnal Korrigan,
a black raven of Morrigan.

A whirling Dervish in Sama,
or a voodoo Haguan or Mama?
I became a drug crazed Korrigan,
A fiery Macha of Morrigan.

A circle has no end or beginning,
Drink the Wine of ecstasy, become part of the living.
I became a youthful Korrigan,
all acts of pleasure are the rites of Morrigan.

Morrigan: I see, you've been busy harvesting!

Corax: Yes and every night I've chanting your chant: *"Morri Morri Morigan. Morigan Sidhe, Morri Awen.".*

Morrigan: Oh that was you! I wondered which irritating b*****d was making all that noise and stopped me from going to sleep every night.

Corax: Yes but you have finally come, so the chanting worked.

Morrigan: No I haven't come because of your chanting, it's Samhain the New Year and I have come for my presents.

Corax: Presents?

Morrigan: Yes, my New Year presents. Come on, where are my presents? Don't tell me you've forgotten my presents....

Corax: Of course not; I would never forget the New Year which is also your birthday and our anniversary. I have put them somewhere around here. *(Looks frantically round the room, talking to himself: "shit I knew I was suppose to buy something today, what the hell am I going to say to her. I need to give her something." Looking under the sofa he finds a yew branch.)*

Corax: Great Queen I have for you a Yew branch, the Yew tree due to its death/rebirth properties is seen as a symbol for Samhain, and its fallen bark or leaves or red berries could be used symbolically. The red berries symbolise the shedding of blood traditional at this time as excess cattle were slaughtered. The seed also holds the potential for the future and coming spring.

Morrigan: That's lovely, how thoughtful of you. Did you plan it for months?

Corax: Oh yes I cut the branch at the full moon near Beltane.

Morrigan: That's great, thank you for remembering my new year, my birthday and our wedding anniversary. It's surprising how many of my sons forget it.

Corax: *(sigh of relief)* As I said I wouldn't forget.

Morrigan: Indeed, however you seem to have forgotten I can read your mind.

Corax: Oh bugger, I am sorry. I was going to Shamansbury's to buy this great golden chalice and large black Cauldron for you today. But I just forgot.

Morrigan: I KNOW you were going to buy me these things and I was looking forward to replacing my chalice and cauldron with your new ones. But you forgot! Being Samhain, I think you need to meet your Ancestors.

Sound of storm, flash of lighting. Morrigan picks Corax up in her claws and places him in her giant Cauldron.

Corax: Dread lord of shadows, god of life, giver of life.
Yet it is the knowledge of death, open wide I pray thee the gates through which all must pass, let our dear ones who have gone before, return this night to be merry with us, and when our time comes, as it must. O thou the comforter, the

consoler, the giver of peace and rest, we will enter thy realm gladly and unafraid, for we know that when rested and refreshed among our dear ones, we will be born again by thy grace and the grace of the Great Mother, let it be in the same place and the same time as our beloved ones, and may we meet and know and remember and love them again.

Morrigan: *(places more wood on the fire under the cauldron, the cauldron is bubbling)* I hope it's not *too* warm (grins)?

Corax: Very funny, how come this Cauldron is bigger on the inside than it looks from the outside?

Morrigan: It's Samhain and the veil between the worlds is thin, hence you can see and communicate with the ones gone before you, though, you might not survive being boiled in the cauldron! Your next incarnation would certainly not forget my Samhain present (grins) he he he.

Corax: There do I see my father,
There do I see my mother, my sisters and brothers
There do I see the line of my ancestors back to the beginning.
They do call to me,
They bid me to take my place among them
In the halls of Valhalah
Where the brave may live forever.
And may we meet and know and remember and love them again.

(Notes: no animals were hurt in this story, don't try swimming in the ocean on your own and do not climb into a boiling Cauldron without parental supervision. The Coven and The Zodiac are the names of night-clubs in Oxford, and Korrigan is the name for Celtic fairy sons.)

Act IV: The Winter Solstice- Alban Arthan: the birth of the sun.

Corax opens his eyes, yet all still is dark. His head is touching his knees, and his arms are hugging his legs which are touching his chest. He tries to lift his head, (bang) ouch!
He bangs his head on something hard. Feeling his way around he seems to be surrounded by something solid.

Corax: I am stuck in the foetal position, in something solid!

Morrigan: You are in an egg, hush go to sleep, you'll wake the others up, its not morning yet unborn one, go to sleep, no need to struggle.

Corax: I feel so tired...

Rain falls, night after night; rivers burst their banks, washing away human castles in the sands. Leaves fall covering the human made metal veins on the earth, and the trains come to a halt. Snow begins to cover the land, most birds have migrated south, and some animals have already begun their hibernation. All life is slowing down, except for the children of clay, who seem to ignore the earth cycle, wanting to keep the same pace of life in all seasons. The seasonal lack of light depression kicks in for some; others increase their caffeine intake to compensate for the slowing of their natural body rhythm.

A month passes, Corax is dreaming of feeding on juicy bull carcasses, and flying high over green lands with the wind under his wing in the summer sunshine.

Morrigan: Corax, time to wake up.

Corax: I am staying here. It's nice, warm, and comfortable.

Morrigan: Well, it might be comfortable for you, but not for me. I have hardly moved all this time trying to keep you eggs warm!

Corax: Can I just stay one more night, please....its so lovely here.

Morrigan: No, time runs differently here, an hour here is a week outside. You have to crack 'your' eggshell open yourself. I carried you within me first, then laid your egg, and then looked after it in the dark winter with my own warmth. I want you to come out now, and don't hide your light.

Corax: If I must, what a shame can't things be like they are now and must 'change'.

Morrigan: Come out; remember your dream earlier, much joy and adventure await you.

Corax: Yes, but so does age, death and decay, shadows and fears. If I come out, I will start the chain again, and die again. Dusk follows dawn.

Morrigan: Between your birth and death lies your journey, your adventure.

Corax: What if this time, I forget your signs and do not recognise you goddess? What if I walked the earth without recognising the sounds of birds as the music of the heavens. What if I forget I ever had wings! What if I swim in the sea and forget it's where all life on earth comes from or breathe the air and forget that every breath is god sent. What if I only saw a lifeless rock instead of the goddess Luna or a just nuclear reaction when I look at the sun? Instead of proclaiming your beauty, and remembering circular time, I might be caught in the linear time, filled with greed to consume time. Take each grain of the sand of time and squeeze every atom out of it, consume everything in my path, dig mines deep into your body, and suck the black blood of our dinosaur ancestors to move my metal coffin, and pay for it in red blood of our distant brothers or sisters. What if I become a destroyer and enslave life, and follow a 'one true way' and slay anything that doesn't conform to my 'one way' and turn the sky black. Nooo! The stakes are too high, I am not coming out.

Morrigan: My child, you have to be true to yourself. Yes instead of becoming a loving daughter or son, you may become a destroyer, and only consume the earth and life and not respect it. But remember I am 'all' life, in my sky vultures, ravens, doves, pigeons and eagles all fly. In the moment of your last enlightenment you declared: 'there is no part of me that is not god', and I replied: 'there is no rain drop that is not of the ocean'.

Corax: I remember so clearly the last time, the time I was a moth, before I became Corax. I would only fly at night and I had the bats to avoid. I had heard from others of the 'midnight sun', a warm bright sun that would only briefly appear in a cave late at night. One night I saw you, the midnight sun, bright beautiful. I flew towards you, not worried about my grey uniform and wings getting muddy in the storm in my rush. I found a way pass the glass window and began circling around you, a candle in the dark night. Free, I could hear the song of the birds once more, and ignored the orders that came. I traced the outline of the cross medal on my uniform, with my finger and I had chosen a Motherland over the Fatherland. You pulled me out my body before the bullets of the firing squad reached me. The fire of the candle consumed me, a little grey moth.

Morrigan: Yet you like 1000 others came back again, and this time you became my Corax. It is time, the dawn of this longest night approaches, my sun is being born. All my little ones like you also need to come out. Come father, brother, consort, son/sun rise.

*From afar, Corax can hear the voices of the **Salmon**, the **Bear**, the **Stag** and the **Hawk**, they are speaking in chorus:*
Queen of the moon, Queen of the Sun,
Queen of heavens, Queen of the Stars,
Queen of the waters, Queen of the Earth,
bring to us the Child of Promise,
it is the Great Mother who gives birth to him,
it is the Lord of Life who is born again,
darkness and tears are set aside,
when the sun shall come up early,
golden sun of the mountains, illuminate the land,
light up the world, illuminate the seas and the rivers,
sorrows be laid, joy to the world,
Blessed be the Great Goddess, without beginning, without end,
Everlasting to eternity, blessed be.

Corax begins to hit his eggshell with his body, until eventually a small crack appears, and bright light falls within the egg.

Corax: The dawn has come; the sun has already been reborn. I must hurry, to greet the sun. I can hear the sound of my brothers and sisters, some are already out of their shells and others are still trying to break free.

Morrigan: Welcome back everyone, your journeys await you.

Corax: *(panic in his voice)* Where are we? Who are all these people in white, why I am covered in blood and why is that lovely lady screaming? She looks just like you but without the wings.

Morrigan: You remember this you have been here before.

Corax: Yes, no, I mean, I remember, oh no I will forget it all if our bodies separate!!! (A nurse with a pair of scissors approaches the mother and baby.)

Corax: I remember it 'all' now, but if the umbilical cord is cut, I will forget it all, until the right time arrives; when the smouldering ash turns to a burning pyre.

Morrigan: My child this is the hardest moment for us both.

Corax: I know and we've been here so many times before (tears flowing from both). What words this time will you bury deep in my mind to help me remember you later?

Morrigan: Four words, Light, Life, Love, Liberty.

Corax: I will remember, Light, Life, Love, Liberty.

(The nurse cuts the umbilical cord, all fades away).

Act V: A Kali Puja: a magickal workshop.

On a bright sunny day, Corax was flying over the forest when he heard the sound of falling trees. He flew to where the sound had originated, and was greeted by sight of his old mate Oilphant Ganesh. Oliphant was gently making his way across the forest, knocking down trees like they were grass, (which to him they were!)

Corax: Hi, you're looking cheerful 2day where r u heading?

Oliphant: Hi, going to new temple in the old castle.

Corax: Not the castle!

Oliphant: Yes, there is a new temple to Kali, and there will be a 'Kali Puja' workshop to mark Kali's festival...

Corax: Wow a real Kali Puja, I always wanted 'to do' a Puja, who is running the Puja?

Oliphant: Its Lady Pelican, she spent a whole six months in India and a year in Siberia.

Corax: Great, I'll accompany you then.

Corax and Oliphant make their way towards the castle, they are faced with signs like: 'keep off the moors' and 'don't go to the castle'. They both shake their heads on such signs muttering about Christians who try to stop them reaching enlightenment. As they approach the castle several hearses leave the gate, carrying coffins. At the door they are faced with a very nice dog called Canine.

Canine: Welcome brothers, and sisters. The workshop is about to start. Just leave all your dosh in the donation box on the way in and please take off your shoes.

Corax and Oliphant excitedly go in and sit down in the large meeting room, which is freshly painted. Corax smells the faint scent of blood underneath the smell of paint.

Lady Pelican: Sit down and relax your body......

Many hours of chanting, and meditation pass, however there is no sign of Kali as far as Corax can see.

Corax: (whispering) Oliphant, can you see Kali?

Oliphant:(whispering) No, except I felt touch of hands on my shoulder.

Corax: Sorry that was me, I was nodding off and had to balance myself by putting my hand on your shoulder.

Oliphant: Oh, well this is just not happening for me, do you remember the door opening thingy that drunk rat told us about the other day in the pub.

Corax: Yep, you mean opening doors to parallel dimensions and letting the gods come through.

Oliphant: Yes, let's try it.

Corax and Oliphant try the 'opening the door thingy' and suddenly the room is filled with flashes of lightning.

Lady Pelican: Keep the chanting going everyone, here comes 'The Goddess'.

One of the ladies, who was already painted in blue stands up and starts handing out flowers to all.
Oliphant and Corax look at each.

Corax: I guess it didn't work, she was already painted in blue!

Oliphant: Errrmmm, look at the ceiling!

A translucent blue figure is forming on the ceiling.

Corax: Uh that would be Kali, though she is not wearing her usual human skull necklace.

Oliphant: She prefers her necklace fresh, probably.

Corax: I am sure it will be fine, where are you going Oliphant? Oliphant?

(Oliphant runs off very quickly).

The rest of congregation seemed to be too busy chanting and collecting the flowers to notice the blue figure descending. The rest happened in a flash, several heads were chopped off by Kali before anyone had noticed. The Kali priestess screamed on seeing Kali and everyone opened their eyes. Kali picks several heads from the floor and makes a skull necklace, which she brings and puts on her priestess.

Kali: You, who act as my priestess, should wear my necklace.

The Kali priestess faints. (Perhaps it was the weight of several human heads dangling from her neck which overcame her.)

Kali: Now for my own necklace.

Kali's blade moved across chopping several more heads, and was approaching Corax fast. But Corax is fixed in his seat, caught by the beautiful light from Kali's eyes. Kali's Blade is inches away from Corax, when it hits another metal object. The sound makes Corax to break eye contact and look up. It seems another blade had stopped Kali's blade. The hands holding the sword are covered in black feathers.

Corax: Morrigan, ace what timing.

Morrigan: Silly boy, I'll deal with you later.

Kali: Get out of my temple Morrigan, this is not your place, can't you see I am busy.

Morrigan: Not this one, he is Mine.

Kali: He is in my temple.

Morrigan: He already belongs to me....

Lots of lightening and sword fighting between Kali and Morrigan takes place.

Corax looks across at the dead bodies, the fainted priestess, and the rest of living congregation and finally sees the workshop organiser Lady Pelican. Lady Pelican seems calm and is handling the situation much better than others. Corax walks up to her.

Corax: Is this what you had in mind for the workshop?

Lady Pelican: Be calm child, we are all in the astral plane now and what you are seeing is a vision, and not real. Remain focused on your breathing.

Corax: Are you sure this is all in the astral plane?

Lady Pelican: Yes and we are now communicating with each other as I have Telepathy Certificate Level 42.

Kali and Morrigan are fighting each other just above the heads of Corax and Lady Pelican.

Corax: (while dodging one of Kali's arms) I see, maybe you should bring this workshop to an end, it seems that Kali and Morrigan are fighting each other.

Lady Pelican: You just focus on the astral vision, and allow it to tap into the collective subconscious, these goddesses are archetypes.

Corax: They seem very real to me, do archetypes chop people's heads off?

Lady Pelican: The chopping off the heads which 'you' are seeing is internal symbol for liberation, also Kali and Morrigan are not really fighting, as you know all goddesses are just one goddess.

Kali and Morrigan suddenly stop fighting, and both look at Lady Pelican.

35

Lady Pelican: As I said. They are all just One Goddess. ... Corax why are you running away?

Corax: But do 'they' know they are all one goddess.

While flying away Corax took one quick look over his shoulder, and saw Kali and Morrigan both with their swords raised rushing towards Lady Pelican. Despite flying away fast, Corax still heard Lady Pelicans screams..... Flying, he quickly caught up with Oliphant, who was also still running.

Oliphant: Glad you made it out, what happen to the rest?

Corax: Death by archetype.

Act VI: Imbolc

Corax: Great Goddess Raven, you look a bit different today.

Morrigan: Really Sherlock.

Corax: Have you done something with your hair?

Morrigan: Well spotted, do you like it?

Corax: Yes, it's lovely, and your feathers have changed colour too, they are white and look like swan feathers.

Morrigan: I know, it's because the first stirrings of spring are about to occur, and the first Plough takes place.

Corax: Look into the mirror of my eyes, and see yourself my goddess, you seem to be changing.

Morigan: I know, the fire is beginning to run in the veins of land and my body, snow is melting and snow drops are beginning to spring forth. This is the time of my step daughter and sister Brigid. She is daughter of the Dagda. She will have her time, as a goddess or a Christian Saint, Saint Brigid of Kildare. My sister is a goddess of poetry, healing and smithcraft, and Brigid's perpetual fire was kept up until the Reformation by the Christian nuns of Kildare. St Brigid was the midwife of the Virgin Mary. The time of Imbolc sees the birth of the first Lambs, and the first signs of spring. She is the Guardian of young children and animals and she is the Keeper of the Flame.

Corax: Sounds very interesting (looking bored), but I feel a bit tired, can I go to bed now.

Morrigan: OK go on then. We'll carry on with your education either tomorrow or in another lifetime.

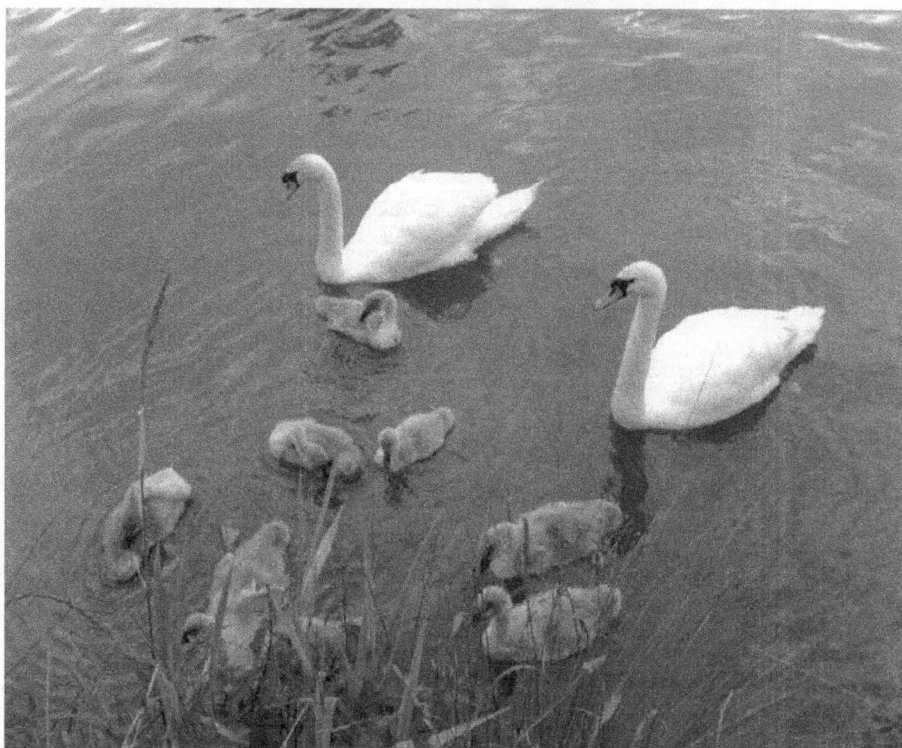

Act VII: The Dance of Death

Morrigan: The problem with astral projection is sometimes you could end up in someone else's body.

Corax: I didn't really believe it could work.

Morrigan: Well it does, and now you are in a bit of a predicament.

Corax looks at the image in the mirror in front of him in the ladies toilet of the night club. Blood red hair, matched up with red corset, black boots and black leather skirt.

Corax: Well this is not what I am used to, gosh red hair! How much dye does she use for this?

Morrigan: Lots. Fyi Corvus is asking me what after shave and deodorant you are wearing?

Corax: It's Voodoo by Lynx. Is Corvus as shocked about this as I am?

Morrigan: Yes, I was just chilling and suddenly I hear you Corax and Corvus thinking about astral projection while both were looking in the mirror, and zap you just swapped. You need to talk to each other about this.

Corax in Corvus's body steps out of the ladies and heads toward to the gents and he/she is met with Corvus in Corax's body, dressed in black leather trousers, bearded, and leather waist coat and of course the smell of Voodoo deodorant. It's strange looking at yourself through someone else's eyes.

Corax: I am not used to walking in heels, I nearly just fell over.

Corvus: Huh, I am covered all over in hair, it would take weeks to wax all this!

Corax: I ...you ....we... need a drink, two large gin and tonics should help.

Corax and Corvus spend some time drinking and discussing all the problems of being in the other's body, until the DJ plays a song which both recognise as being one of their favourites. Both rush to the dance floor. It's weird dancing with yourself, but slowly all the advantages of being in the other body come into mind, and hormones starting kicking in.

Corax and Corvus starting dancing with each other or is it Corvus and Corax.

Its getting stranger as slowly both become aroused from dancing with each other. Both can hear Morrigan giggling somewhere overhead about their situation. Nature is taking its course; Corax and Corvus start French kissing. Bizarre feeling your own tongue in your own mouth kissing you back....is this really getting off with yourself or someone else. As the kissing continues, the dance floor slowly melts away, Corax and Corvus are snogging and dancing in middle of a giant nest on top of an ancient tree, near edge of a cliff. The tree is covered in bones, skulls, feathers, and coloured ribbons (the skulls probably belong to those who foolishly came and tied the ribbons to the tree). A red sunset dominates the sky, and the smell of rotten flesh fills the nostrils (probably an improvement to the Lynx deodorant). The distant drum beat is echoing in the valley. Or is it the music from the night club....Kissing lends itself to gently stroking of each other's body, their black wings slowly begin to open from their shoulders. They rise slowly, somewhere between the earth and the sky, and their bodies begin to entwine, like ivy climbing stone columns. The serpents of caduceus. Engulfing. Flames rise from their bodies as they beat their wings faster and fly higher. As a bright white shooting star flies across the sunset red sky, and falls on the earth, Corax and Corvus reach their Nirvana.

As the bliss begins to pass Corax and Corvus feel themselves fall down again, this time into their original (rather wet now!) bodies.

Morrigan: You two better have another gin and tonic before the next song starts!

Act VIII Beltane 4play

Corax: Ummm, mmmm, eeooeprps

Morrigan: What?

Corax: Ommmmumm nnnmmmopmm

Morrigan: What? Didn't anyone ever tell you, you shouldn't really speak with your mouth full? Wait let me move myself. (She lifts herself from Corax's face).

Corax: I was trying to say, I've one of your feathers stuck between my teeth and can't breathe.

Morrigan: Well just remove the feather.

Corax spits the feather out and pushes aside the feathers on
Morrigan's yoni as she descends on his face once more.
Suddenly Corax realises why magick is called an oral tradition.

Act IX: An eclectic pagan's near-death experience

On a clear winter day was Corax was happily feasting on
remains of a mouse in someone's garden, gently tearing away
the half rotten flesh and eating it, when suddenly a cat jumps
him. Claws and beak meet each other, fur and feathers flying
away, Corax thinks to himself "is it my time? Was I destined to
die today? Did I want to be attacked today?" Too much
thought really for the heat of battle and a heavy blow from
the cat almost knocks Corax out, before passing out he aims
for the cat's eyes and then blackness.

He is floating up, and after few minutes he sees a bright
tunnel, and there is light at end of the tunnel, (he wonders if
it's a oncoming train!) but no, the whole tunnel is becomes
light. He is drawn in and flies into the tunnel of light.

After a while he reaches end of the tunnel and is greeted by Morrigan.

Morrigan: Well you seem to have died, time for a walk on the other side, and follow me my child.

Another tunnel of light appears and Morrigan is about to lead Corax through. When another tunnel of appears from nowhere and a group of men in full Roman armour march out, part of a Roman Legion.

Antonius: Nama Corax time to join our rank in afterlife, in the fields of Elysium.

Corax looks at his comrades on one hand and Morrigan on the other, and wonders where would be more fun to spend eternity. A loud voice breaks his thinking...

Duir: Greetings!

Corax sees origin of the voice being from a new tunnel of light, standing in front of it an old man with white beard holding a golden sickle and next to him a woman with numerous blue woad paintings on her body.

Duir: Follower of the wooden door and yew bark, follow us, it's time for you to become a seedling in our grove, grow slowly and turn in due course and many a life times to a great oak.

Corax is beginning to feel uncertain, which tunnel of light should he go into? Where to spend eternity? Suddenly loud laughter grabs his attention, a tall black man with face painted white; wearing a top hat and sun glass comes through another door and tunnel.

Baron Samedi: Ha Corax, here drink from this bottle of Rum. Your time has come, come with me and you might even become a Loa. You'll be remembered, and have dances made to you.

Another voice even louder, from yet another tunnel appears. A bald man with a 666 tattoo on his forehead points a finger at him.

Crowley: Do what thou Wilt, you are not dead or alive, and there is nothing beyond your will. Afterlife is but an extension of your Will.

Another voice: 'Dream on' says a black spider whose web spans the starry night.

Arachne: Don't worry Corax about being eaten by me, you'll be reborn as star in the night sky, you have always been star dust, no more, no less.

Corax looks at the gathered assembly, even more uncertain where to spent eternity, after all eternity is a long time! Another tunnel appears, and he can see the Great Pyramids over the horizon, and temples of Abydos and Luxor. Shining brightly Isis, Osiris, Horus, Thoth, Seth, Sekhmet et al, all looking amazing and inviting.

A priest appears holding a pair of weighing scales: Corax it's time to have you heart weighed against this feather. Then you may swim in the life giving Nile.

From above he hears sound of horses, and looks up and sees several armour clad warrior women on white horses.

Valkyres: Come Corax you died in battle with a cat, mead and eternal rejoicing await you.

Another door, opens to the sound of 'Om Namah Shiva', Lord Shiva approaches holding his trident.

Shiva: Corax the ever youthful Ashrum of knowledge awaits you; let Kali bring you across the threshold to us.

Yet another door appears, Corax sees his grand parents, they seem have more feathers, like in their youth.

Grandmother: Corax it's time to rejoin your family in your village.

Another door opens and from it comes, a man holding a cross:

Jesus: Remember I died for your sins heaven or hell awaits you.

"Ignore all this" **says another voice.**

Nietzsche: Remember what doesn't kill you makes you stronger, I guess on this occasion it killed you, and now you are just worm food.

From above yet another door opens "Garrh, garrrrh" descending like a black cloud come a flock of ravens, the Great Raven Spirit, of whom each raven is but a feather on her giant body.

Great Raven: Come Corax time to fly with us and roam the astral plane.

Corax looks at all the tunnel of lights, and doors, thinking its probably going to take sometime to decide where to go.

Corax: This is great, where the f**k do I go from here, and eternity deciding where to go.....

Morrigan: Well what do you expect, eclectic in life eclectic in death....... I wonder perhaps you should go back and make your mind up..

Corax finds himself back in the garden, the cat is moving away with a sore eye. Corax has lost few feathers, but is still alive, to fly for another day.

Act X: Beltane

Morrigan: Reader, I married him.

Act XI: *Justice for the RollRight Stone Circle*

Oliphant Ganesh bumps into Corax in the woods, who is carrying a baseball bat.

Oliphant Ganesh: Namaste Corax, where are you going with that baseball bat?

Corax: I am going to give my mate Karma a hand.

Oliphant Ganesh: <u>U</u>mmm...are you sure?

Corax: Well sometimes, you need to speed Karma up. Full respect to cockroaches, but if they spray yellow paint on Morrigan's nest, well a baseball bat up the b****m certainly helps them to see the error of their ways.

Oliphant: Well that's not so tolerant of you? What happened to all that love, light and saying 'be kind' to all?

Corax: I am being kind, that's why I have tube of KY jelly for the bat.

Oliphant: I see, well let's go and give Karma a hand.

(Note: The RollRight Stone Circle in Oxfordshire is an ancient stone circle of great beauty, however over the last few years there has been number of vandals repeatedly damaging it.)

Act XII: Living like the pagan ancestors

Deep in the woods, in a hut surrounded by silver birch trees, the 'Pagan Woodcutters' moot is taking place. The beer, wine, mead and spice are flowing. Oliphant, Corax, Bovine, Duck, and Pelican are all sitting and chatting about living like their pagan ancestors.

Bovine: It would be great to live off the land, to farm it like our ancestors, to dig and plough from dawn to dusk. To be close to the land and see it transform as seeds turn to wheat.

Oliphant: Yeah, or plant fruit trees, and then pick them.....

Pelican: Or live in caves, with the central fire, and go hunting.....

Corax picks his beak from the wine glass. Thinking to himself: bugger breaking one's back on ploughing a farm from dawn to dusk, or spending all day in any weather condition picking apples, or live in a smelly smoky cave and then run around with a bloody spear to get dinner.

Duck: It would be great to just live on the beach living off fishes.

Corax thinks well maybe but bloody mosquitoes, and did Duck never watch 'Lord of the Flies' or Castaway...anyway you can't just live off fish, your body needs other foods too.

Duck: Well Corax, would you like to live like your pagan ancestors?

Corax: Yes, it would be great to live like my pagan ancestors; I would be living in my Roman Villa looking out onto green vineyards. Sitting in my reclining seat on the marble balcony and being fed grapes and sipping wine produced from my own vineyard. The spa and warm baths are only around the corner, the chariot race on Saturdays; followed by a Roman orgy in the evening. Yes, I think I could manage to live like the pagan ancestors.

Act XIII: The Towers of Silence

It is dinner time and Morrigan is leading her children to supper.

Morrigan: What does everyone fancy tonight?

Corvus: How about going for French cuisine I hear the Gaulish temples in Northern France are full of decaying bones, especially Ribemont has some lovely offerings, you can even get Duir Burgers™ made from the Bulls meat offerings.

Morrigan: They have nice roof platforms for the bodies to decompose, but the bodies are still wearing armour, which gets in my beak.

Corax: They swap the upper parts of the bodies with lower parts at the waist, very tasty each body is made of two persons really, a bit like a Big Mac, but they lack the head so we won't know the expiry date.

Corvus: Well, how about going for an Indian, a spicy curry would help me to digest the last of the Greek meal we had last week.

Corax: I did say remove the wrapper (toga) before eating.

Corvus: Well at least I finished my meal, you left half of yours.

Morrigan: Ok children that's enough, stop arguing. This week we go for an Indian and next week for a French one. Both happy? Good, and Corax how many times I told you, always finish your food.

Morrigan and her children begin their flight to Bombay for an Indian meal, the Zoroastrian 'Tower of Silence' restaurant used to be a global Franchise at one point but now only a handful (beakful) remain. The quality of food is still good but being in the middle of a city now the food is smoked, which gives a strange after taste.

Morrigan: Now remember kids you must not drop any of the food in the city, and avoid the planes when going over the airport.

Corax and Corvus exchange a mischievous glance.
On their arrival, they are met with an elderly man, a Nasarsarlas, who greets them with their names.

Morrigan: Greetings to you too, I'll have my usual table please; you haven't changed at all from my last visit.

Nasar: Great Queen, that was my grand father, it's been many years since your last visit. I have the three towers ready as always, the deceased men in the outer circle, women in the middle circle and children in the inner circle.

Morrigan: Thank you, I think I'll sit at the inner circle; Corax will eat the middle circle and Corvus the Outer Circle.

With that the three begin their feasting. Soon all are full and Morrigan decides to have a siesta. The kids are also full and begin playing with their food, and soon they are flying all over the city with remains of their meal.

Corax accidentally drops a skull in someone's swimming pool, while Corvus accidentally drops a leg on top of a bank. It doesn't take long before its raining bones, and the whole city is in commotion; some also land in a Kali Ashram. Kali doesn't like to be woken up by piece of ribcage (unless it's her own chest clock made by 12 Raja's skulls). She sticks her head out and sees Corax doing a Maradona's 'Hand of God' impression by pushing someone's skull straight into a bus stop full of people.

Kali: Oi Corax! What do you think you're doing?

Corax: Ummm Auntie Kali, didn't realise you were in.

Kali: Don't Auntie Kali me; you know the rules, never play with your food! And don't drop them in the city. Where is my sister?

Corax: Morrigan is having a nap.

Kali: Not after the racket you two have been making, here she comes now.

Morrigan: CORAX, CORVUS, what the Hel have you two been up to?

Kali: Look at the mess they made, the whole place is covered in body parts.

Morrigan: Honestly Corax and Corvus it's this sort of behaviour that caused the decline of most of the Celtic cults of decomposition. Your behaviour could cause this fast food tower to be closed as well.Go and clean up the mess you created, and return all the bones to their original place.

Corax: Yeah, but no, no but yeah but no....

Morrigan: Just get on with it NOW!

Act XIV: The Magi's gifts

Corax was flying over Carfax tower in Oxford when it started raining heavily, so he began to look for shelter avoiding the Christmas lights, which were in his usual flight route in the High Street. He headed towards Christ Church, being Christmas Eve, all the lights of the Cathedral were on.

He made a circle over the Hermes' statue in the quad, seven times out of respect, and then flew to sit on ledge of one of the great windows of the Cathedral. He was just getting comfortable when he noticed the Hermes statue was waving his caduceus at him! Corax was a bit surprised by this and despite the rain he flew and landed on the statute.

Hermes: Glad you saw me wave, I've got a message for you from Morrigan.

Corax: Really? I am not late for dinner am I?

Hermes: No, well I don't know, anyway, the message is to be at main gate to guide 3 visitors to the Bishop's office.

Corax: Uh, ok. Who are the visitors?

Hermes: They are the three magi.

Corax: Why are they coming?

Hermes: Don't know, got to dash, remember midnight at the gate.

Corax was wondering why the three Magi would come here tonight. No one makes 2000 years of time travel unless they have a good reason. He found the main gate and waited till midnight. On the 12th stroke of the great clock, suddenly three shapes appeared, their red Phrygian caps were the first thing anyone would have noticed, the cap of liberty of the magi, the sign of those whose souls were freed, their red cloaks billowing in the wind, their baggy trousers also catching the wind.

Corax flew and sat on shoulder of one of them, they said nothing. No words were needed, Corax guided them to the main door of the cathedral, and they knocked three times and walked straight in.

The midnight mass was in full flow when the three strangely attired men, with a raven on the shoulder of one them wandered in. Rev Shepherd was taken aback by the sight and stopped in mid mass. The congregation turned to look. The three walked straight up the aisle without looking at anyone. They even ignored the Rev and seemed to head towards what was the nativity set made by local schools showing the virgin birth scene with Mary, baby Jesus and the three magi bearing gifts.

The three walked onto the set and proceeded with what could be described as dismantling part of it. Rev Shepherd seemed to come out of shock finally and made a dash towards them.

Rev: Excuse me gentlemen what do you think you are doing? Stop now.

They ignored him and continued to take apart part of the set, well the part that had the three magi in it. They picked up the plastic gold, myrrh and frankincense and the dolls representing themselves and started to head out.

Rev: I must protest, you are damaging this set.

First Magi: No, we are just taking back our gifts, the gifts were meant to be for all mankind and Jesus' message was kindness. The Church has abused our gifts and ignored His message.

Second Magi: We travelled far to be at his birth as we had high hopes for this star of Bethlehem. You had your chance.

Third Magi: We are taking our gifts to another place and time.

With that, they walked out of the Church.

Corax (*Looks at the Christ on the Cross*)**:** Are you staying or coming?

Jesus: I am not hanging around here either.

With that he climbed down from the cross and headed toward the Magi to leave with them.

Corax: Any of you Saints staying?

Mary was already getting ready to go and several of the saints were also coming out of the stained glass windows to head out. Within a few minutes, all were following the Magi out of the Church.

Rev Shepherd was in shock again....

As the three Magi, Jesus, Mary, Joseph and a number of saints gathered outside of the Church.

Corax was beginning to wonder what they are going to do next, especially seeing how cold and wet it was and none had dressed for winter. Sandals are fine in Bethlehem but not for the winter in the UK!

One of the Magi seemed to have noticed the cold too, and he appeared to be ordering 12 shish kebabs from the kebab van, hot food would keep all of them warm. Jesus quickly turned some of the rainwater into wine. So all were drinking wine and eating kebabs soon while discussing what they should do.

Mary: Look there is a number 1 bus, why don't we catch it to Temple Cowley and camp in the Knight's Templar's sanctuary, Baphomet will be glad to see us.

First Magi: Corax, make sure they get to the Knight's Templar's temple, we are off in a different way, we need to take the gifts back.

Minutes later the Magi disappeared, they went in the westerly direction, while Corax, Jesus, Mary, Joseph and several saints headed east toward Temple Cow-Ley.

It was going to be strange Xmas, and it was only 1am....

That's all folks!
The End.

Disclaimer: All places, events and all characters in this play are fictitious and any resemblance to any one alive or dead is purely accidental.

* 9 7 8 0 9 5 5 6 8 5 8 0 4 *